Thoughts of Krishna

Thoughts of Krishna

A book of bhakti poetry

Chandra-Vadana Chaitanya das

Jackson

indirectknowledge.com

Contents

1

Introduction

Please accept my humble obesiances! All glories to Shrila Prabhupada!

This is a small book of poetry I wrote during my daily meditations with the Lord. I don't know how others will find reading these poems but they were meaningful moments for me. I hope if nothing more readers will be encouraged to give up something material for something spiritual.

When you love someone, a personality, whatever, you serve that someone from the heart. You serve them regardless if they reciprocate. You serve them for no other reason than besides the fact you love them. That's all.

Like with someone, something, etc., we can love God the same way. We can offer every action as an offering to God. We can serve in every capacity we can so long as that service comes from the heart.

When we serve and it is not in our heart to do so, perhaps we're motivated by some other reason, we suffer and feel resentment. Service should always be from the heart, motivated by no other reason besides love alone.

I hope you enjoy the poetry.

Haribol,

Chandravadana Chaitanya das

1

I Love You Krishna

Krishna, you are the embodiment of love,
You fill my heart with your divine presence.
I am so grateful for your infinite love and light,
Which guides me through each and every day.
Your love is the light that guides me home,
And I am so blessed to be loved by you.
Thank you for always being there for me,
showering me with your endless love.

Krishna

Krishna, the blue-skinned deity
Is often portrayed playing the flute
His haunting melodies lure us to him
As we surrender to his divine will
He is the lord of love and compassion
The protector of the innocent and virtuous
May his presence fill our hearts with joy
And bring us closer to our ultimate goal

3

My Krishna

Krishna is the divine one
He is the lord of love and light
He is my guiding star
He brings me hope in the dark night
His love knows no bounds
He is the answer to all my prayers
I am so grateful for his love and care

4

Another Day with Krishna

Another day with Krishna
Is a day well spent
He brings so much happiness
And love to our lives
He makes everything feel so worth it
Every time we're together
Just being in His presence
Is like finding true heaven

5

Fill My Heart Krishna

Krishna, divine lord of love
Fill my heart with your grace
Envelop me in your infinite mercy
For I am nothing without you
Guide me on my path to salvation
And show me the way to final freedom.

Early Mornings with Krishna

Early mornings, I awaken to find
Krishna by my side, in all his divine glory
I can't help but be mesmerized by his radiant form
As he smiles serenely and speaks softly to me
I am filled with an inner peace and joy
For these brief moments, I am one with the divine
And all my worries and concerns seem far away
In the company of Krishna, I am content

7

The Moon Light Casts a Pale Light

In the night sky,
the beautiful moon shines.
In the night sky,
the beautiful moon shines.
The moon light casts a pale light,
illuminating the dark night sky.
Amidst the stars,
the moon is a bright light.
Krishna dances in the moon light,
casting his bright light on all around him.

Krishna's Beauty is a Riddle

    Krishna by the water,
Blue and beautiful,
You smile and I am drawn to you.
I want to come close,
But you slip away.
Your beauty is a riddle,
I can't solve it.
But I'm happy just to stare
At your form by the water.

9

Krishna and the Gopis

Hear the tales of Krishna and the gopis
He stole their hearts with his love divine
They would follow him anywhere
Their love was true and pure
There was nothing like it before or since
Krishna was their star, their guiding light
They worshipped him with all their might
He brought them happiness, joy and love
None could compare to his precious gift
Forever they will remember those blissful days
When they were with Krishna and the gopis
His love is something that will never die
It is etched in their hearts forevermore.

Radha Krishna

Krishna was so handsome
And the gopis loved him so
But he only had eyes for Radha
The loveliest of them all
No matter how hard they tried
The other gopis just couldn't compete
For Krishna's love and attention
They were happy just to be near him
And listen to his sweet voice
Radha was the one he chose
To be his eternal love

Sleeping Krishna

It's 10:36 at night and all is still
The moon casts a gentle light
Down upon the earth and all who dwell
Krishna sleeps, as all around him wind whispers soft
His dreams of love and compassion sure to bring delight
In the morning he will awaken and once again bring
Light into the lives of everyone he meets

Distribute Books for Krishna

Krishna Book Distribution is the best way
To serve our lord and savior
It's a great opportunity to share
The love and wisdom of Krishna
You can bring happiness to others
And it's a really good feeling too
So join in and do your part
And help spread the word of Krishna

13

Cooking for Krishna

I am so happy to be cooking for Krishna
I know He will enjoy every bite
I am going to prepare a feast fit for a King
With love and devotion in my heart
I know He will be pleased
It is an honor to cook for Him
And I am so grateful that He allows me to serve Him
His Holy presence fills my kitchen with light
And I am filled with joy as I cook for my Lord.

Gaura and Nithai

Installing Gaura and Nityai,
the process is so meticulous,
the results are so beautiful,
and the deities so dear.
First the altar is prepared,
then the mantras are sung,
while the sacred fire is burning.
The images of Gaura and Nityai
are then consecrated with water, milk, honey and ghee,
and finally the devotees offer their prayers.

15

Radha's Sadness

I can't stop crying thinking of Krishna,
The love of my life and my everything,
My thoughts are consumed with him night and day,
I hope one day he will come back to me.
I cry all the time because I miss him so much,
I wish I could just see him one more time,
I would give anything to just hear his voice,
Krishna, please come back to me!

Krishna Maha Mantra

Krishna Maha Mantra
This mantra is so potent and pure
It brings great peace and liberation
When chanted with faith and focus
Krishna will surely bless you
His divine presence entering your heart
And empowering you to live with purpose
Be devoted to this mantra and be blessed

Reading About Krishna

Reading about Krishna, I feel my heart fill with love.
He is so divine, a true vision of beauty.
I can't help but feel happy when I think of him.
His teachings give me hope and illuminate the way.
I am grateful for the gift of his teaching and his presence
in my life.

18

Krishna's Smile

Krishna's smile brings the night sky to life
With a billion stars shining bright
He makes the dark blue hue appear
And bring peace and love to all who hear.

19

Krishna's Love Gives Way to Day Anew

Krishna's love is like the sun
It fills the sky with blue
And all the darkness it dispels
Gives way to day anew
His love is so all encompassing
It touches everything we see
The night sky is no exception
It becomes alive with light and energy
With Krishna's love in our hearts
We can face any darkness head on
And know that the dawn will come soon
Bringing happiness and joy once more.

20

Srila Prabhupada

Srila Prabhupada, an extraordinary guru,
Humble yet powerful, a true saint.
He brought Hare Krishna to the West,
And taught us how to love God.
His teachings are pure, simple and profound,
And through him we can experience Krishna.
Thank you Srila Prabhupada for your divine instruction,
For your understanding and compassion,
And for showing us the path to enlightenment.

Krishna's Devotees

When Krishna shines down on earth
All His devotees feel His love and mirth
They follow Him with all their heart
Never wanting to be parted
They sing and dance with great joy
Filled with happiness and love

Krishna's Devotees #2

The devotees of Krishna are a special breed
They have found the love and devotion that leads to everlasting peace
Their faith is unbreakable, their love is true
And they will follow Krishna wherever He may lead
Their hearts are pure and their minds are clear
They have left behind the worries of this world
For they know that through Krishna they will find salvation
They serve Him with all their hearts and souls
And they will never forget the kindness He has shown them
They are the lucky ones, who have been given a chance
To be close to Lord Krishna and worship Him forever.

Krishna's Devotees #3

Krishna's Devotees are so special,
They love Him with all their hearts,
They follow His teachings and example,
And always try to please Him.
By doing puja and chanting Hare Krishna,
They make their lives more meaningful,
And they know that simply being near Krishna,
Is the ultimate happiness.

24

Krishna's Devotees #4

There is something about Krishna's devotees
That sets them apart from all the rest.
They have a light in their eyes
And a joy in their hearts
That is truly unique.
No matter what life throws their way,
They remain devoted to Krishna.
Their faith is unshakeable,
And they are always ready to serve Him.
They are a special breed of people,
Who have chosen to dedicate their lives to Krishna.
They are role models for the rest of us,
And we can learn a lot from them.

25

Krishna's Bhagavada Gita

The Bhagavada Gita is a sacred text
That guides us on the path to salvation
It teaches us how to control our mind
And renounce the material world
    Krishna is its author and perfect teacher
He explains the philosophy of Vedanta
And reveals the way to liberation
    Through self-knowledge and devotion to God
We can overcome all obstacles in life
And achieve true happiness and peace.

26

Krishna Supreme Lord

Krishna is the Supreme Lord
He is the origin of all that exists
He is the one who pervades everything
And yet He is infinitely more
He is the source of all knowledge
And the destroyer of all ignorance
He is the bringer of salvation
And the dispenser of divine grace
Lord Krishna, I offer you my heart and soul
Please bless me with your love and mercy

Krishna, Playful Prankster

Krishna, the playful prankster,
Always making everyone smile,
His infectious laughter ringing through the air,
Oh how we all love him so!
His eyes as bright as the sun,
His skin as dark as the night sky,
He is the most beautiful being we have ever seen,
And we are so blessed to call him ours.

28

Krishna The Demon Slayer

Krishna, the dark God with cow's ears
And flute in hand, eternal lover of Radha
Born to slay demons and rescue the pious
He leads us in song and dance across the land
His divine grace is ever present
In him we find boundless love and joy
O grant us your mercy, Lord Krishna!

Hare Krishna

Krishna is the all pervading Lord
He is the supreme absolute
One who chants His name is sure to be liberated
Hare Krishna Hare Krishna
Krishna Krishna Hare Hare
Hare Rama Hare Rama
Rama Rama Hare Hare

Hare Krishna #2

Hare Krishna, Hare Krishna
Krishna Krishna, Hare Hare
Hare Rama, Hare Rama
Rama Rama, Hare Hare
    chant these names and feel their power
fill your heart with love and devotion
step into a new way of life

I Can't Help But Sing Hare Krishna

I cannot help but sing of Hare Krishna
His names are many, like the stars in the sky
He is the absolute, without beginning or end
The source of all creation and its destroyer
The sustainer of all life and the dear friend of all creatures
Hare Krishna, Hare Krishna, Krishna Krishna, Hare Hare
Hare Rama, Hare Rama, Rama Rama, Hare Hare

Mantra Forever

Hare Krishna Hare Krishna Krishna Krishna Hare
Hare
Hare Rama Hare Rama Rama Rama Hare Hare
This simple chant is so profound
It brings us all to the eternal abode
of Lord Krishna
Where we can enjoy His divine company forever

Lord Chaitanya's Nama Sankirtana

Hare Krishna Hare Krishna Rice and beans and roti
Kirtan and meditation How we love to sway
days go by in blissful joy with Lord Caitanya
Nama sankirtana is the music of our hearts

Krishna's Arrives in Vrindavana

Krishna arrived in Vrindavan wearing a dhoti,
His long, dark hair cascading down his back.
His blue eyes sparkled with love and laughter,
And the people of Vrindavan were enchanted.
He danced and played with the children,
And they loved him with all their hearts.
The women of Vrindavan were drawn to his beauty,
And they admired his grace and charm.
Krishna is the perfect example of a perfection

35

Krishna's Dhoti

   Krishna is the lord of all,
The wearer of the dhotis bright,
Who shows us truth and love,
And brings us closer to the light.
   He dances in the fields of Vrindavan,
His laughter ringing out clear,
As he spreads his love around,
Bringing peace and happiness near.
   The dhotis that he wears so well,
Are symbols of his grace and might,
They bring us wisdom and joy,
And help us find our way in life.

36

Chaitanya's Teachings

Sri Chaitanya is the incarnation of Lord Vishnu
He is the Supreme Personality of Godhead
He came to this world to preach love of God
He is the ocean of mercy and compassion
He is the bringer of spiritual enlightenment
His teachings are the highest truth
Everyone who follows His teachings will be saved.

37

Radha Krishna Prayer

My heart is filled with love for Radha Krishna
The divine couple who make my life complete
They bring joy to my heart and light to my path
I can't imagine life without them by my side
Their love is eternal and I am so blessed
To have them in my life, I offer my prayer

38

Real Love

They say that God is everywhere,
But I think he must have been in Vrindavan
When Radha and Krishna were together.
Their love was so pure and true,
It makes my heart feel light and happy.
I can't imagine what it must have been like,
To witness their divine love firsthand.
Radha and Krishna are the perfect example
Of how real love never dies.

Simply Serving Lord Krishna

There's a joy in serving Krishna
It's a love that fills the heart
When we render selfless service
We feel his love and mercy start
To flow like a sweet river
Carrying us away to realms divine
Where we experience pure bliss
And eternal happiness is ours
Simply by serving Lord Krishna!

Krishna Sadhaka

Krishna Sadhaka,
Thou who art the perfect example
Of one who has dedicated himself to spiritual practice,
Lead us on the path of truth and enlightenment.
Help us to find the inner peace and happiness
That comes from union with the divine.
Grant us the strength to overcome all obstacles
On our journey to liberation.

I Want to Serve Krishna More

I want to love Krishna more
I want to please Him more
I want to give my love to Him unreservedly
I want Him to be my everything
I want to serve Him with all my heart
I want Him to be the focus of my life
And I want to spend eternity in his company

Supreme Krishna

Krishna is the Supreme Lord
He is the embodiment of love
He has unlimited compassion
He has all qualities of goodness
He is the source of all spiritual knowledge
He is the giver of liberation
He is the Supreme Personality of Godhead
I offer my love and devotion to Him

43

Krishna Krishna Krishna

    Krishna, the most divine
Infinite love and compassion
Our hearts melt when we see your face
Radiant light burning with grace
Incredibly beautiful, you are the one
We constantly long to be with